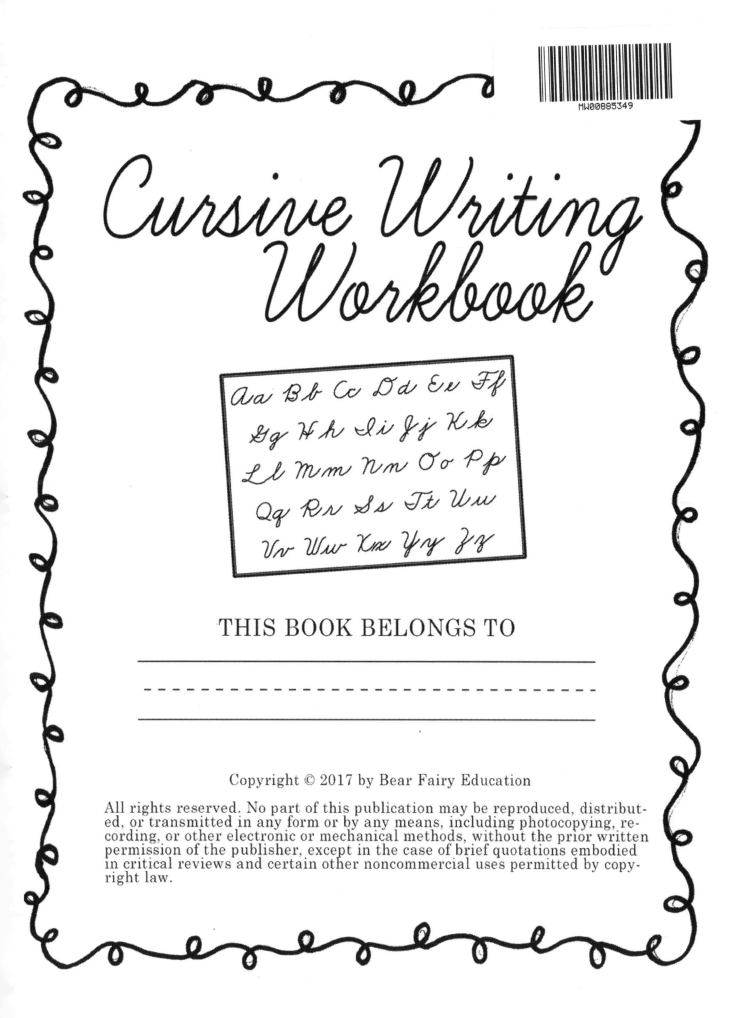

Cursive Writing Workbook

Aa Bb Cc Dd Ee Ff
Gg Hh Ii Jj Kk
Ll Mm Nn Oo Pp
Qq Rr Ss Tt Uu
Vv Ww Xx Yy Zz

THIS BOOK BELONGS TO

_____

- -

_____

Write the word for the picture you see.

Trace the sentence and then write the sentence.

WRITE THE WORD FOR THE PICTURE YOU SEE

bee

bear

TRACE THE SENTENCE AND WRITE THE SENTENCE.

The bee and the

bear were friends

The bee and the bear

were friends

C C C C C C

C C C C

U U U U U U U

c c c c c c c

C c

WRITE THE WORD FOR THE PICTURE YOU SEE

cupcake

cat

TRACE THE SENTENCE AND WRITE THE SENTENCE.

Can a cat eat a

cupcake?

Can a cat eat a

cupcake

D D D D D

D D D D

d d d d d

d d d d

WRITE THE WORD FOR THE PICTURE YOU SEE

Dog

door

TRACE THE SENTENCE AND WRITE THE SENTENCE.

My dog sat at

the door.

$\mathcal{E}$ $\mathcal{E}$ $\mathcal{E}$ $\mathcal{E}$ $\mathcal{E}$ $\mathcal{E}$

e e e e e e e

$\mathcal{E}$ e

WRITE THE WORD FOR THE PICTURE YOU SEE

TRACE THE SENTENCE AND WRITE THE SENTENCE.

The eagle laid an egg in the nest.

$\mathcal{F}\ \mathcal{F}\ \mathcal{F}\ \mathcal{F}\ \mathcal{F}$

$f\ f\ f\ f\ f\ f\ f\ f\ f\ f$

WRITE THE WORD FOR THE PICTURE YOU SEE

TRACE THE SENTENCE AND WRITE THE SENTENCE.

The fox jumped over the fence.

$\mathcal{G}$ $\mathcal{G}$ $\mathcal{G}$ $\mathcal{G}$ $\mathcal{G}$

g g g g g g

WRITE THE WORD FOR THE PICTURE YOU SEE

TRACE THE SENTENCE AND WRITE THE SENTENCE.

I took my gloves to pick grapes.

$\mathscr{H}$ $\mathscr{H}$ $\mathscr{H}$ $\mathscr{H}$ $\mathscr{H}$ $\mathscr{H}$

h h h h h h

$\mathcal{H}\,h$

WRITE THE WORD FOR THE PICTURE YOU SEE

TRACE THE SENTENCE AND WRITE THE SENTENCE.

My heart is in your hands.

ℓ ℓ ℓ ℓ ℓ

i i i i i i i

I i

WRITE THE WORD FOR THE PICTURE YOU SEE

TRACE THE SENTENCE AND WRITE THE SENTENCE.

We ate ice cream

in an igloo.

Jj (cursive letter tracing practice)

WRITE THE WORD FOR THE PICTURE YOU SEE

TRACE THE SENTENCE AND WRITE THE SENTENCE.

I ate jelly from the jar.

K K K K K

k k k k k k

K k

WRITE THE WORD FOR THE PICTURE YOU SEE

TRACE THE SENTENCE AND WRITE THE SENTENCE.

I lost my kite
and my key.

$\mathscr{L}$ $\mathscr{L}$ $\mathscr{L}$ $\mathscr{L}$ $\mathscr{L}$

ℓ ℓ ℓ ℓ ℓ ℓ

WRITE THE WORD FOR THE PICTURE YOU SEE

TRACE THE SENTENCE AND WRITE THE SENTENCE.

The ladder was

went to the lamp.

$\mathcal{M}$ $\mathcal{M}$ $\mathcal{M}$

m m m m

$\mathcal{M}$ m

WRITE THE WORD FOR THE PICTURE YOU SEE

TRACE THE SENTENCE AND WRITE THE SENTENCE.

The man ate

The muffin.

N N N N N

N N N N N

N n

Catch that fish

with your net!

O O O O O O

o o o o o o

WRITE THE WORD FOR THE PICTURE YOU SEE

TRACE THE SENTENCE AND WRITE THE SENTENCE.

An octopus lives in the ocean.

P P P P P P

p p p p p p

P p

WRITE THE WORD FOR THE PICTURE YOU SEE

TRACE THE SENTENCE AND WRITE THE SENTENCE.

A penguin can't

eat popcorn.

$\mathcal{Q}$ $\mathcal{Q}$ $\mathcal{Q}$ $\mathcal{Q}$ $\mathcal{Q}$

q q q q q

$\mathcal{Q} q$

WRITE THE WORD FOR THE PICTURE YOU SEE

_____

_ _ _ _ _ _ _ _

_____

TRACE THE SENTENCE AND WRITE THE SENTENCE.

The queen slept

with a quilt.

R R R R R

r r r r r r

R r

WRITE THE WORD FOR THE PICTURE YOU SEE

TRACE THE SENTENCE AND WRITE THE SENTENCE.

I raked leaves

under the rainbow.

$S\ S\ S\ S\ S$

$s\ s\ s\ s\ s\ s\ s$

WRITE THE WORD FOR THE PICTURE YOU SEE

TRACE THE SENTENCE AND WRITE THE SENTENCE.

The snail likes the sun.

$\mathcal{T}\ \mathcal{T}\ \mathcal{T}\ \mathcal{T}\ \mathcal{T}$

$t\ t\ t\ t\ t\ t\ t$

$\mathcal{T}t$

WRITE THE WORD FOR THE PICTURE YOU SEE

TRACE THE SENTENCE AND WRITE THE SENTENCE.

The turtle sat under the tree.

𝒰 𝒰 𝒰 𝒰 𝒰

𝓊 𝓊 𝓊 𝓊 𝓊

𝒰 𝓊

WRITE THE WORD FOR THE PICTURE YOU SEE

TRACE THE SENTENCE AND WRITE THE SENTENCE.

𝒯𝒽𝑒 𝓊𝓃𝒾𝒸𝑜𝓇𝓃 𝒽𝒶𝒹

𝒶𝓃 𝓊𝓂𝒷𝓇𝑒𝓁𝓁𝒶.

$\mathcal{V}$ $\mathcal{V}$ $\mathcal{V}$ $\mathcal{V}$ $\mathcal{V}$

v v v v v

V v

WRITE THE WORD FOR THE PICTURE YOU SEE

_____

TRACE THE SENTENCE AND WRITE THE SENTENCE.

Did you see the

Volcano explode?

Uu Uu Uu Uu

w w w w

WRITE THE WORD FOR THE PICTURE YOU SEE

_____

_____

TRACE THE SENTENCE AND WRITE THE SENTENCE.

Look at the time

on your watch!

$\mathscr{X} \quad \mathscr{X} \quad \mathscr{X} \quad \mathscr{X} \quad \mathscr{X}$

$\mathscr{X} \quad \mathscr{X} \quad \mathscr{X} \quad \mathscr{X} \quad \mathscr{X} \quad \mathscr{X}$

WRITE THE WORD FOR THE PICTURE YOU SEE

TRACE THE SENTENCE AND WRITE THE SENTENCE.

I like to play a xylophone.

$\mathcal{Y}$ $\mathcal{Y}$ $\mathcal{Y}$ $\mathcal{Y}$ $\mathcal{Y}$ $\mathcal{Y}$

y y y y y

$\mathcal{Y}\,y$

WRITE THE WORD FOR THE PICTURE YOU SEE

_____

- - - - - - - - - - - -

_____

- - - - - - - - - - - -

TRACE THE SENTENCE AND WRITE THE SENTENCE.

Do you like yarn and yo-yos?

WRITE THE WORD FOR THE PICTURE YOU SEE

TRACE THE SENTENCE AND WRITE THE SENTENCE.

Zebra and zipper start with "z".

a a a a a

a a a a a

$\mathcal{B}$ $\mathcal{B}$ $\mathcal{B}$ $\mathcal{B}$ $\mathcal{B}$

b b b b b

$\mathcal{D}$ $\mathcal{D}$ $\mathcal{D}$ $\mathcal{D}$ $\mathcal{D}$

d d d d d

$\mathscr{F}\ \mathscr{F}\ \mathscr{F}\ \mathscr{F}\ \mathscr{F}$

$f\ f\ f\ f\ f$

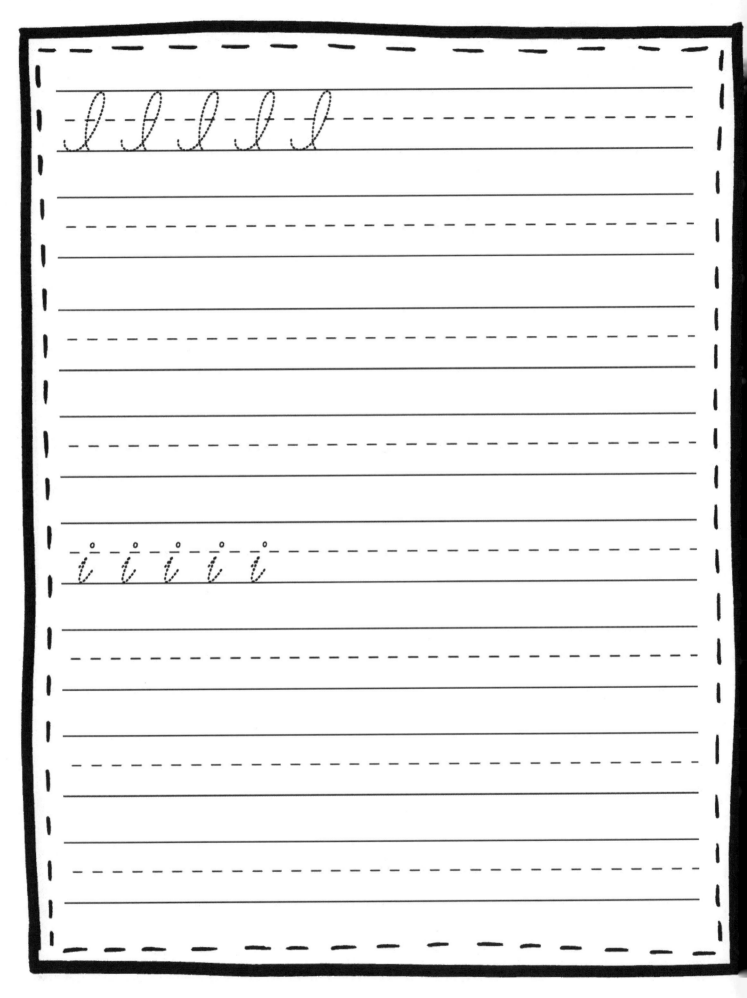

m m m m m

m m m m m

N N N N N

n n n n n

p p p p p

p p p p p

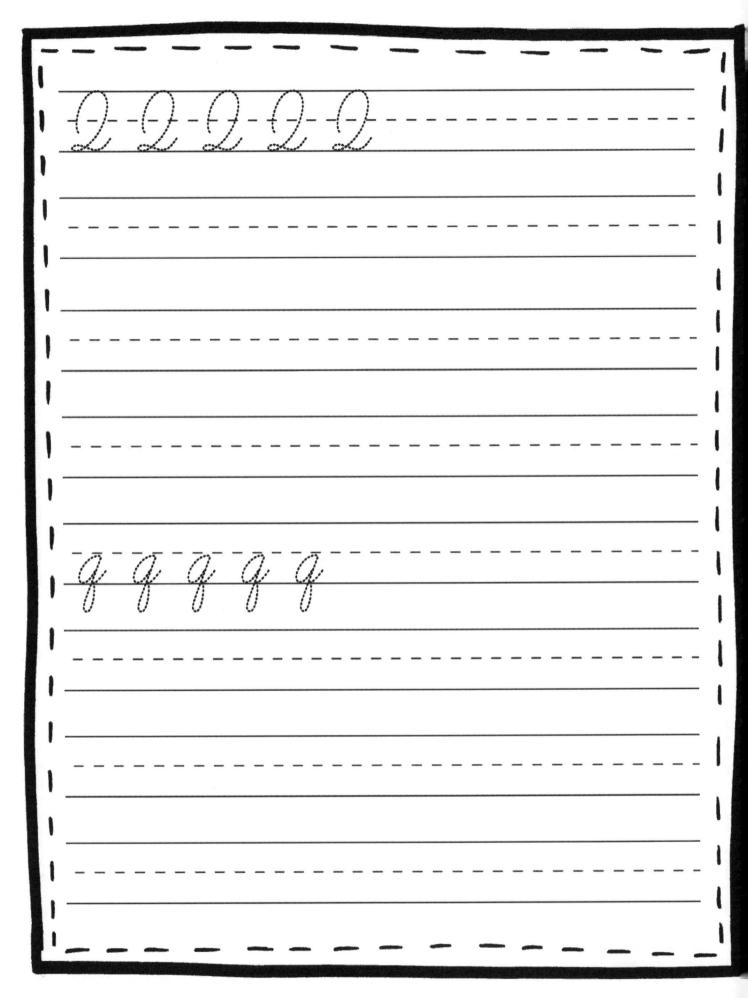

Monday

Tuesday

Wednesday

Thursday

Friday

Saturday

Sunday

January

February

March

April

May

June

July

August

September

October

November

December

7 CONTINENTS

North America

South America

Europe

Asia

Africa

7 CONTINENTS

Australia

Large land masses are

called continents. There

are seven continents on

planet Earth. The largest

continent in size is Asia.

NUMBERS

one

two

three

four

five

six

seven

NUMBERS

eight

nine

ten

eleven

twelve

thirteen

fourteen

NUMBERS

fifteen

sixteen

seventeen

eighteen

nineteen

twenty

COLORS

Red

Blue

Orange

Green

Black

Pink

Yellow

SPORTS

Basketball

Football

Baseball

Volleyball

Dance

Golf

Soccer

TRACING A-Z

TRACING A-Z

a b c d e f g

h i j k l m

n o p q r s

t u v w x

y z

Made in United States
Orlando, FL
16 May 2023

33196156R00040